WORST OF THE WORST

AIRPLANE CRASHES!

by Aaron Sautter

CAPSTONE PRESS
a capstone imprint

Published by Capstone Press, an imprint of Capstone
1710 Roe Crest Drive, North Mankato, Minnesota 56003
capstonepub.com

Copyright © 2026 by Capstone. All rights reserved. No part of this publication may be reproduced in whole or in part, or stored in a retrieval system, or transmitted in any form or by any means, electronic, mechanical, photocopying, recording, or otherwise, without written permission of the publisher.

Library of Congress Cataloging-in-Publication Data is available on the Library of Congress website.

ISBN: 9798875244810 (hardcover)
ISBN: 9798875244766 (paperback)
ISBN: 9798875244773 (ebook PDF)

Summary: Discover history's worst of the worst aviation events, including the tragic disappearance of Malaysian Airlines Flight 370, the terrorist attacks of 9/11, and more. From midair collisions to technical failures and pilot errors, uncover the causes and consequences of crashes that changed the way we fly.

Editorial Credits:
Editor: Donald Lemke; Designer: Tracy Davies; Media Researcher: Svetlana Zhurkin; Production Specialist: Whitney Schaefer

Image Credits:
Alamy: Album/Archivo ABC, 11, BFA/Netflix, 9; Associated Press: 7, 19, Fred Jewell, 13, Steven Day, 25; Getty Images: byggarn79, 5, Corbis/robert wallis, 17, Hulton Archive/Evening Standard, 8; Newscom: EyePress Newswire/FL Wong, 29, Sipa Press/Michael Schwartz, 21, Sipa/Halim Berbar, 28, TNS/Chicago Tribune/Michael Laughlin, 12; Shutterstock: Arc Tina (plane icon), spine and throughout, Bjoern Wylezich, 15, FedBul, cover, Lionel Alvergnas (explosion design element), cover and throughout, Lukas Gojda, 4, Makajin (clouds design element), cover and throughout, Markus Mainka, 27, Steve Heap, 23, VVadi4ka (torn paper), cover and throughout; U.S. Department of Defense: Air Force Tech. Sgt. Cedric H. Rudisill, 22

Any additional websites and resources referenced in this book are not maintained, authorized, or sponsored by Capstone. All product and company names are trademarks™ or registered® trademarks of their respective holders.

Printed and bound in China. PO 6459

TABLE OF CONTENTS

Words in **BOLD** are in the glossary.

INTRODUCTION

DISASTER IN THE AIR

SCREECH! A terrible noise fills the airplane. *BANG!* An engine bursts into flames. *VRRRRR . . . BLAM!* The plane streaks toward the ground and explodes.

Airplane crashes are horrible events. They often kill many people. Sometimes they cause a lot of damage. Buckle up! It's time to discover some of the worst of the worst airplane disasters.

CHAPTER 1

MIRACLE IN THE ANDES

DISASTER FACTS

Flight: Uruguayan Air Force 571
Date: October 13, 1972
Location: Andes Mountains, Argentina
Lives Lost: 29
Survivors: 16

Several members of a rugby team lived a nightmare in 1972. They were on a **chartered** plane to Santiago, Chile. But it never arrived. It crashed in the Andes Mountains. Several people were killed in the disaster.

The remains of Uruguayan Air Force Flight 571

But that was just the start of the story. The survivors were stuck high in the mountains. Many were injured. They soon ran out of food.

To survive, the living had to eat the dead. After two months, three men left to find help. The remaining 16 survivors were finally saved about ten days later.

Three survivors of the Uruguayan Air Force Flight 571 crash

The 2023 film *Society of the Snow* details the true story of Uruguayan Air Force Flight 571.

FACT!

The survivors' dramatic story has been told in several books and feature films.

CHAPTER 2

TRAGEDY AT TENERIFE

DISASTER FACTS

Flights: KLM 4805, Pan Am 1736
Date: March 27, 1977
Location: Los Rodeos Airport, Tenerife, Canary Islands
Lives Lost: 583
Wounded: 61

Two planes began to take off on the same runway. But it was very foggy. The pilots didn't see each other in time. One tried to turn, but it was too late. The planes crashed and exploded. More than 580 people were killed. It was the deadliest airport disaster in history.

FACT!

Dense fog and bad radio communications were blamed for the crash. Both pilots mistakenly believed they were cleared for takeoff.

CHAPTER 3

DISASTER AT O'HARE

DISASTER FACTS

Flight: American Airlines 191
Date: May 25, 1979
Location: O'Hare International Airport, Chicago, Illinois
Lives Lost: 273
Wounded: 5

Investigators sift through the wreckage of American Airlines Flight 191.

In 1979, tragedy struck in Chicago, Illinois. A large plane lost its left engine as it took off. The plane tilted sideways in the air. Then it crashed in a huge fireball. Everyone was killed. Two people on the ground also died. It was the worst airplane accident in U.S. history.

FACT!

A memorial to the passengers and crew of American Airlines Flight 191 is located near the crash site.

CHAPTER 4

FIRE IN THE SKY

DISASTER FACTS

Flight: Saudia 163
Date: August 19, 1980
Location: Riyadh, Saudi Arabia
Lives Lost: 301

BEEP! BEEP! BEEP! Smoke alarms warned of a fire in the plane's **cargo hold**. The captain made an emergency landing. But the plane's engines were not shut down right away. Rescue crews could not get to the airplane. It was soon full of **toxic** smoke. All 301 people on board died.

The Saudi Flight 163 disaster involved a Lockheed L-1011-200 TriStar aircraft.

FACT!

The fire on Saudia Flight 163 was the deadliest airplane disaster not involving a crash.

CHAPTER 5

TRAGIC TAIL FAILURE

DISASTER FACTS

Flight: Japan Airlines 123
Date: August 12, 1985
Location: Mount Takamagahara, Japan
Lives Lost: 520

In 1985, many people were flying for the Japanese holiday Bon. But disaster soon struck. A sudden **decompression** damaged the plane's tail. The captain lost control. The plane slammed into a mountain. All but four people were killed. It was the deadliest single-plane disaster ever.

Japan Airlines Flight 123 crash site

FACT!

In 1978, an accident had damaged the plane's tail. Experts believe that flawed repairs led the tail section to fail, causing the plane to crash.

CHAPTER 6

HORROR AT 24,000 FEET

DISASTER FACTS

Flight: Aloha Airlines 243
Date: April 28, 1988
Location: Maui, Hawaii
Lives Lost: 1
Wounded: 65

It was supposed to be a normal trip. But then something unexpected happened. Part of the plane's roof tore off! One flight attendant was blown out of the plane. Many people were injured by flying **debris**. The captain managed to land the plane. Amazingly, only one person died in this scary accident.

Medical teams treat injured passengers of Aloha Airlines Flight 243.

FACT!

It was found that small cracks around rivets in the plane's **fuselage** had caused it to fail.

CHAPTER 7

TERROR STRIKES ON 9/11

DISASTER FACTS

Flights: American Airlines 11 and 77,
United Airlines 175 and 93
Date: September 11, 2001
Locations: New York City; Washington, D.C.;
Shanksville, Pennsylvania
Lives Lost: 2,977
Wounded: more than 6,000

It was a quiet morning in New York City. But that soon changed. A large airplane smashed into the World Trade Center's North Tower. Fire and smoke filled the sky. Soon, a second plane slammed into the South Tower. Before long, both towers fell into huge piles of rubble. More than 2,700 people were killed.

Terrorists had **hijacked** the planes. They also took over two other planes. They crashed one into the Pentagon in Washington, D.C. Later, the fourth plane crashed in Pennsylvania. Everyone on both planes was killed. The attacks of September 11 were the deadliest air disaster in U.S. history.

The crash caused major damage to the Pentagon.

Tower of Voices monument at the Flight 93 Memorial in Shanksville, Pennsylvania

FACT!

Experts think the terrorists wanted to crash Flight 93 into the White House. But the passengers fought back, and the plane crashed in a Pennsylvania field instead.

CHAPTER 8

A TRICKY LANDING

DISASTER FACTS

Flight: US Airways 1549
Date: January 15, 2009
Location: New York City, New York
Lives Lost: 0
Wounded: 5

Passengers in New York got a fright in 2009. After taking off, their plane ran into a flock of geese. The plane's engines were badly damaged. Captain Chesley "Sully" Sullenberger had to make a risky decision. He landed the plane on the Hudson River. A few people were injured, but nobody died.

Survivors stand on the wings of US Airways Flight 1549 while awaiting rescue.

FACT!

As the plane floated on the river, the passengers and crew waited on its wings to be rescued.

CHAPTER 9

LOST AT SEA

DISASTER STATS

Flight: Malaysia Airlines 370
Date: March 8, 2014
Location: Southern Indian Ocean
Lives Lost: 239

Can a big airplane simply disappear? That seemed to happen to Malaysia Airlines Flight 370. On its way to Beijing, China, the plane's **transponder** was switched off.

An airplane similar to Malaysia Airlines Flight 370 takes off.

The crew also stopped radio communications. **Radar** showed the plane turning and flying west. But then all contact was lost.

Authorities believed the plane crashed in the Indian Ocean. They searched a remote area southwest of Australia. But the plane was never found. Over time, 27 pieces of debris washed up on beaches around the Indian Ocean. The mystery of the doomed flight may never be solved.

Rescue teams search the South China Sea for the missing plane.

Family members look at crash debris during a remembrance ceremony in 2020.

FACT!

The search for the missing plane involved 33 ships, 58 aircraft, and cost more than $150 million.

GLOSSARY

cargo hold (KAHR-goh HOLD)—the part of a ship or plane where goods are carried

charter (CHAR-tuhr)—to hire (as a ship or a bus) for temporary use

debris (duh-BREE)—the remains of something that has been broken or destroyed

decompression (DEE-kum-preh-shuhn)—loss of pressure inside a sealed aircraft

fuselage (FYOO-suh-lahj)—the central body portion of an airplane that holds the crew, passengers, and cargo

hijack (HY-jak)—to force a pilot to fly an aircraft where one wants

radar (RAY-dahr)—a device that uses radio waves to find the location and distance of an object

toxic (TAHK-sik)—poisonous

transponder (tran-SPAHN-duhr)—a radio that sends back a signal when it receives one, often used to track airplanes

READ MORE

Luján, Jarred. *Planes in Peril.* North Mankato, MN: Capstone, 2025.

McCollum, Sean. *Fighting to Survive Airplane Crashes: Terrifying True Stories.* North Mankato, MN: Capstone, 2020.

Romero, Libby. *September 11.* Washington, D.C.: National Geographic, 2021.

INTERNET SITES

History.com: Miracle of the Andes: How Survivors of the Flight Disaster Struggled to Stay Alive
history.com/news/miracle-andes-disaster-survival

Britannica Kids: Mount Erebus Disaster
kids.britannica.com/students/article/Mount-Erebus-disaster/633217

National Geographic Kids: Remembering September 11
kids.nationalgeographic.com/history/article/remembering-september-11

INDEX

ABOUT THE AUTHOR

Aaron Sautter is an author and editor of dozens of cool books for young readers. He enjoys a wide range of subjects from dramatic history and sports to spooky aliens and fantastic creatures. Aaron lives in Minnesota with his wife and two children. In his spare time, Aaron enjoys cheering for the Minnesota Vikings and going for long walks with his goofy, lovable dogs.